TRIAL OF A JUDGE

by Stephen Spender

TRIAL
OF A JUDGE

a tragedy
in five acts

Faber and Faber Limited
24 Russell Square
London

First published in March Mcmxxxviii
By Faber and Faber Limited
24 Russell Square London W.C. 1
Printed in Great Britain by
R. MacLehose and Company Limited
The University Press Glasgow

Trial of a Judge was written for the Group Theatre, and first produced by Rupert Doone with décor by John Piper.

To

T. A. R. H.

The world wears your image on the surface
And judges, as always, the looks and the behaviour
Moving upon the social glass of silver;
But I plunged through those mirrored rays
Where eye remarks eye from the outside,
Into your hidden inner self and bore
As my self-love your hopes and failure,
My other self for which my self would have died.

Drowned in your life, I there encountered death
Which claimed you for a greater history
Where the free won, though many won too late.
We being afraid, I made my hand a path
Into this separate peace which is no victory
Nor general peace, but our escape from fate.

CHARACTERS

The Judge
The Judge's Wife
Hummeldorf
Petra's Mother
Petra's Brother
The Fiancée
A Communist (Third Red)
Five Black Prisoners (Black Chorus)
A Fascist Troop Leader
Two Fascists (Sixth Black and Seventh Black)
Jewish Doctor Prisoner
Chorus of Red Prisoners

ACT I

ACT I

ILLUSION AND UNCERTAINTY

[SCENE: *The edge of a wood in the garden of the Palace of Justice. Through the trees are discernible the lights of the Palace and the Square on to which it faces. Lights and colours suggesting illusion and uncertainty. Action suggesting that this act is a dream in the Judge's mind.*]

[*Enter the* JUDGE, *from the trial in which he has just passed the death sentence on Petra's murderers. He is agitated. Dressed in court robes.*]

JUDGE. 'Regret,' let me remember, 'Regret.'

What did I speak? 'Regret.'

Every word was true. Not one word

Does my conscience take back.

Yet to call murder murder is a kind of killing,

Perhaps which makes me their souls' murderer.

The carotid artery was severed,

Petra's body mangled out of recognition.

What could I say, except assert

That my famous gentleness, changed to outrage,

Would stamp their lives out with a kind of pleasure?

13

'Judge not, lest ye be judged'—that means nothing,
    I suppose,
Unless that, in killing, judges may not damn men's
    souls
—Old tags echo in the ear.
Even the masked frock-coated executioner,
With his naked surgery, kills but judges not.
The surgeon should have hands to pity
Gangrened flesh the scalpel cuts.
Yes, yes; but what I said I disposed over their exe-
    cution
Not to their souls but at their deeds
To a listening world which must be warned.
Why do I remember these things? I suppose
A lawyer's a man well-trained in memory
Of cases, precedent, repartee, speeches,
So now my words like birds fly after me.
What did I say? 'Regret.'

    [*Savagely, echoing not the words but the impli-
    cation of his speech to the Court, he turns round
    and addresses an at first invisible* CHORUS, *who
    gradually come forward from under the trees,
    until they stand round, facing him, as much the
    accusers as the accused. The whole scene vaguely
    recalls the arrangement of the Court. The* JUDGE
    *stands on a slightly higher level of the proscen-
    ium.*]

We are driven to violence by violence
Of groups hidden in crowds, like a ripe core
Packed with black seeds driving outwards.

You have loosed inciting leaflets: with crimes
Done under covering night, you would melt
All confidence in rules to one searing rule
Of organized terror. You know the law
Makes hourly statements like electric advertise-
    ments
In city squares—those man-tall golden letters
You have stood in falsely with false legality
When practising sharp-shooting at the edge of woods
—When severing the life of this Jew.
I do regretfully
Announce a change made in the law
Which, acting retrogressively, makes political
    murder
Punishable with death:
Regret. Let me remember, regret.
No, I am glad.
To stamp you out, we will change the laws to traps
In every street
Common as traps of drains under your feet.

[*The* BLACK CHORUS *is composed of Five
Prisoners. They are too idealised to be dismissed
simply as bullies; yet they suggest at once the
accused and the accusers, the oppressed and the
oppressors. First, their voices mutter in the
background, as though they were a memory in
depths of the Judge's own unconscious mind.
Later, they come to the front of the stage, until, at
the end of the scene, they stand between the audience and the* JUDGE.]

15

FIRST BLACK PRISONER. Our orders were to shoot
        Petra.

JUDGE. [*as though recalling the voice of the Prosecutor*].
        Who ordered you?

SECOND BLACK PRISONER. We met each night
    Where we could wear our uniforms, in our own
        cellars,
    And there with the town's list before us, we
    Pricked every name of Pole or Jew.

THIRD BLACK PRISONER. Petra came first: he was a
        Polish Jew.

FOURTH BLACK PRISONER. And a Marxist as well.

FIRST BLACK PRISONER. We met on Thursday night
        and motored out
    From Beuthen to Potempa by the road:
    Skidding—spark-showers at corners—we did not
        hug
    The cover of blackness, but as we
    Do here, and always shall do,
    Awakened dumb houses with our slogans
    And let the fumbling secret lovers know
    Loving is trash to those who strike a light
    Of liberating fire with their revenge.

FIFTH BLACK PRISONER. The gross-lipped fawn-eyed
        nigger-skinned
    Hook-nosed intellectual Petra
    Snored in a stenching windowless
    Sty with his mother and his brother.

FOURTH BLACK PRISONER. In unmanly filth of
        poverty, he lacked

Food, candle and fire.
Inferior of physique, he coughed
His guts out, whilst about the room he crept
And wove his plots from sterile cleverness.
To judge from books and papers spread around,
Petra was like an angel, without food
Existing singly from his light of mind.

FIFTH BLACK PRISONER. We dragged him screaming
    Out of the straw bed by the heels.
    I shot him, stripped. Then we stamped on him
    And kicked his face in.

SECOND BLACK PRISONER. Although we thought he'd
          coughed up all his blood,
    When we struck him, there was enough blood.

JUDGE. O, let collectors and doctors recognise
    Here a rarity, like Pandy's disease.
    The carotid artery was severed
    Such violence is a diamond.

THIRD BLACK PRISONER. If you want proof
    That him alone we abhorred as a spy
    And murdered through our racial privilege, remem-
      ber
    We spared two witnesses
    His lunatic mother and his brother.

FIRST BLACK PRISONER. Europe is a jungle where
        the tiger
    Vegetable silence breaks
    —A sun through branches.
    As the spurned ground of all earth's disk
    Which man advancing tramples,

B   17

Slaying grass, axing forests, blasting rock,
Rejecting the inanimate as trash,
So are weak men to the strong.
Soft waters sift away whole soils,
Sentimental moons madden the dogs,
And the effeminate Jew rustling subtly
Through corridors as a brook through reeds,
Our strength saps.

FIFTH BLACK PRISONER. But we are slayers,
  springing
Upon the weak from topmost branches,
Killing the okapi, the kid, the pascal lamb.

FIRST BLACK PRISONER. Let the biped stand, let the
  nordic
Sunhaired head be matched against cloud drifts
And the whip hand crack the lightning
Canine and eye teeth laugh in the sun's face.
His flags never dip except for night
Or their momentary mutual salute
Or to utter surrender—yet Western Man
Less proud than happy standards of bunting
Is barked by dogs, governed by servants,
Gutted by the Jew, reproached by niggers.
Return, O gentlemen of the field, to your primary
  hunting!

JUDGE. Since once in my country
Such a murder is done, and there are eleven million
Who will applaud the doers, we approach
Smoking fields of chaos where
The integral mind melts in collected

18

Panic and cruelty. Standards of justice topple like
    masts
And what's called right seems a battered tin
On banks of rubbish where lie
Flanges of history's once competent machines.
Regard today
Whose paper figure on the calendar
Has shaken the traditional libraries
And still will wing like seed into the ground
To produce from the instant a generation of chaos
Unless some signal act of anger
Strike out these words of murder . . .
To fortify my will
I summon Petra's mother and his brother.

FIFTH BLACK PRISONER. The words of Poles, who,
    when our country
    Knew defeat

FIRST BLACK PRISONER.   —the barriers smashed

SECOND BLACK PRISONER. The soldiers in rags, the
    young hollow-boned,
    The coinage a torrent, our credit dust,
    Crept in to eat our ruin.

THIRD BLACK PRISONER. And the words of Jews——

FOURTH BLACK PRISONER. Their roots suck our
    mines, our factories

FIFTH BLACK PRISONER. Our girls, our boys, our
    industry,
    They secretly channel our blood abroad
    While their gaping mouths as red as our wounds
    Hover in cars or plaster our cafés.

Fourth Black Prisoner. And the words of Com-
      munists——

Third Black Prisoner. Machines without a nation:

Fifth Black Prisoner. Millions of bodies the same:
      millions of minds
Colourless as the Asiatic plains.

Chorus of Black Prisoners. No, we are young and
      die for it, but
The patriot who loves his field shall flourish.
He will plant his wheat with the same hand
As drives aggressors from his land.

Judge [*prosecuting, as before*]. Let
The dead man's brother and his mother speak.
      [*Enter the* Mother *and* Petra's Brother.
      *The mother, a Catholic, wears long nunnish
      mourning. Petra's brother, is in mechanic's blue
      dungarees.*]

Mother. Are you the Judge? Sir, will you discover
The murderers of my son?

Judge [*raising her with a gesture which is really his own
      self-pity*].
Is this woman then a Jewess?
      [*Answering in his rôle of prosecutor, as before.*]
No.
Her room
Carpetless
Lightless bare walls
Smelling of stale cardboard
Was papered
With photographs

20

Of holy paintings and images
Cut from the newspapers.
Is it true, Frau Petra, as these prisoners declare,
    that your son was an atheist?

MOTHER. Now God has forgiven him.

PETRA'S BROTHER. Oh——

JUDGE [*prosecuting, as before*]. Tell us how your son
    came to die!

MOTHER. We went to bed early, for my son was a good
    son
Causing me no anxiety with late hours but staying
    at home;
Going to rest at dark and rising to read by the dawn
He was what you might call a studious one.
Now I pray God to pour Hell fire upon his murder-
    ers
Who, with a dark lantern—five there were—
Broke in with sticks and revolvers on our slumber
—Found nothing to steal except my solitary trea-
    sure
My son, my son. Sir, well I remember
That night, the hottest night of this summer, how
He coughed, so that if at all of evil I dreamt,
It was to pray he might die peacefully.

PETRA'S BROTHER. These five broke on our sleep. I
    thought
They were drunks. When I leapt up
To save my brother, one's leaded truncheon
Dazzled my eyes with a blazing star.
That the harm they planned my brother

21

Was worse than drunken play turned brutal
You all can witness.

> [*Here* TWO ATTENDANTS *reveal the body of
> Petra laid out on a table under lamps.*]

MOTHER. Once this pale-faced child, my son, the slag
    hill
Each morning climbed, serious with his satchel.
He was mature and gentle, like a girl.

PETRA'S BROTHER. Do not—as beggars do—
Hold his wounds under their noses
And change him entirely to horror, pity or frank
    money.

MOTHER. His touch was the last companion for such
    wish
I have for life left in decaying flesh——

PETRA'S BROTHER. Oh
So far from gentle, he is the danger
His murderers and those who gave them orders
Still fear. They did not kill to kill
My already dying brother, stoned
By starvation, hunger heavier
Than a grave's alleviating weight of soil:
For visibly he belonged to dark
Death, like lean tendrils
Of sunless plants, prophesying shroud worms.
They shot only his face
That's still the face of what he is:
Their leaden bullets against a knife edge
Of steel, have tried to turn the blade:
But instantly when he died, the entire knife

Of what he thought and strove, glued to my hand.
He's dead. His living was one word
Influencing surrounding speech
Of a crowd's life, printless until
The words of all this time are frozen
By all our deaths into the winter library
Where life continually flows into books.
For us the blood still melts
We breathe a ripe or sparse or torturing air
And are the cursive act of history
Moving with fever, like distraction
In waves. I with dead sight
Of him you killed—with his undying will
Your bullets shot at—read
In your faces and your actions
Present history, and, in the reading, I shall write.
Myself a word amongst existing words
Reading your words, I see in them death's orders.
I tell you, this impartial judge
Weaker than his own justice, shall smile
And pardon Petra's murderers.
These prisoners, Petra's murderers,
Shall sit upon a bench to judge this judge;
And where my brother's life has printed
The contradiction to your world of lies
I'll stamp his truth again with my own breath,
Yes, even with my death.

MOTHER. Please do not heed him, he's dangerous,
But hear all our history, how we are harmless.
My husband was a Jew and it was twelve years ago

23

That, being hated there, we left Poland, our country.
My two sons were then children whom the migrat-
ory train
Carried crawling inside, with other emigrants,
through
Freezing smoke of that winter night. We experi-
enced
Not kindness, not death, but many small daggers
First of frost, then of hunger, through our bodies.
The mournful telegraph wires which watched our
travelling
From town to town have never worn birds
To sing our harvest in: secret eye never watched us
Profit from this country's loss to become the right
target
For hatred of those who now hit us. Gentlemen,
You who carved furrows through my son, as waste-
fully
As if one intolerable night of flight
Had passed with engine wheels not over his mind
alone
But also across his sensible eyes——
Oh, had you leave now to analyse his ruined flesh
You would find his bones marrowless from a starved
childhood,
His blood impure as your country's debased cur-
rency.
Suffering's suffrage had balloted him
That alas chose the people of our new-chosen
country,

24

Has driven them mad now in their hatred of
strangers.

... If you have any pity, spare a shilling for me.

[*Exit, walking slowly across the stage past the*
Chorus, *who at once revile her and contemptu-
ously throw a few coppers.*]

Judge. Here in the Court of my mind, I invoke
Not only Petra's murderers and the mother
Of him and his brother, but her
Who carries in her body his child.

[*Enter* Fiancée *at back of stage, high up (at the
same level as the balcony in Act III and the
gables in Act V), under smothered rays from the
Palace. She is small, pretty, fair, dressed in a
skirt and red woollen jumper. The* Judge *stands
to the front of the stage, apart, as he watches her
and* Petra's Brother *speak together.*]

Fiancée [*to* Petra's Brother]. I will be the mother
of your brother's child.

Can you take care of me?

Petra's Brother. I must go away.

Fiancée. Where will you go?

Petra's Brother. To follow Petra.

Fiancée. Petra is dead.

Petra's Brother. The frontier which I cross is that
Bombed impassable road within
Easy reach of trained machine guns, which
Divides banks and cathedrals from the slums.
Look up where wealth's Gibraltar stares across
The workers' salt undifferentiated, fretting sea.

There the rich build in simple stone which holds
Cells of our blood and sweat transformed to gold;
And yet I thought all men were kind, until
Their naked guns blasted my brother.
Dear, where I must go I'll go alone
To suffer no morbid wounds from seeing
A home and children starve. I must be poor.
To cross that frontier all I need declare
Is I have nothing and I give my life
To those with nothing but their lives.

FIANCÉE. I'll follow you, although we snatch our peace.

PETRA'S BROTHER. From death, from death——

JUDGE [*apart at front of stage*]. The lovers on their light
and subtle hill,
The dancers in the stage's polished window,
Are buried in my boyhood's memory.

FIANCÉE. Between death and life
Our love shall create a link.

PETRA'S BROTHER. Yes, curled in your body, my
brother's child.

FIANCÉE. We'll tear love——

PETRA'S BROTHER. From the iron assertions of the
time——

JUDGE [*apart*]. They turn like little wheels of clocks:
the hair spring
Girl circling around her central jewel
The trigger sir, the arrow regulator

FIANCÉE. Between the slogans of comrades——

PETRA'S BROTHER. After the ten hours' day in the
factory——

26

JUDGE [*apart*]. O, their wishes were horses on which I
    rode!
  I awaited fulfilment from the sexual rose
  When all the choric petals were unfurled.
FIANCÉE. We'll force love——
PETRA'S BROTHER. To grow in improbable places——
FIANCÉE. Under the street doorways——
PETRA'S BROTHER. The yawning railway arches——
FIANCÉE. One night of release in the park——
PETRA'S BROTHER. Under the trees blossoming with
    electric flowers——
JUDGE [*apart*]. If there is love or any dancer's art
  To restore symmetry now, it must be stronger
  Than small brass wheels—I must have cranes
  To lift stone weights, or love
  Powerful enough to run a country on.
PETRA'S BROTHER and FIANCÉE.
  Petra's child will be fruit of our will.

  [FIANCÉE *and* PETRA'S BROTHER *turn to
  go. Before they do so, whilst she is turned away
  from the stage, he speaks in an impassioned
  voice.*]
PETRA'S BROTHER. Here I have a voice impas-
    sioned,
  Here I have a life disputed and indignant,
  Here I have a message, here I have a life.[1]

  [*Exeunt* PETRA'S BROTHER *and* FIANCÉE.

---

[1] Aquí tengo una voz enardecida,
    aquí tengo una vida combatida y airada,
    aquí tengo un rumor, aquí tengo una vida.
                                    Miguel Hernandez.

The JUDGE *stands over Petra's corpse and
addresses the* CHORUS *with the ritualistic passion
of the law.*]

JUDGE. After the war, after the years of starving, after
chains
    That weighed us down with debt,
    We look across the gulf of chaos,
    Of sporadic fire, wastrel opinion
    Armed with guns: there, responsibility
    Alone of burdens, was fallen from us.
    But now I say at last the change is rung
    Whoever having authority
    Errs from the centre of collected powers
    Pointed into the State, is friend to murderers
    And to that wandering outward fringe of rebel
    Disintegrators.
    The law is better guns and prisons
    Than cracks across our country's discipline.
    Therefore my ruling is that death,
    As ordered by the decree, fall on you.

CHORUS OF BLACK PRISONERS. The people hear our
voice
    The people will change this sentence and make sen-
tences
    Other than this.

JUDGE. The corpse of Petra is a witness
    His wounds are mouths speaking red words.

FIRST BLACK PRISONER. The life of Petra was an
ulcer
    We cut out of our country's body.

JUDGE. The son-deprived womb of Petra's mother
       The fatherless womb of his unborn child
       Cry that their love was murdered.
SECOND BLACK PRISONER. The Jew-bearing womb
           of Petra's mother
       The Jew-debauched womb of his bride
       Were the theatres of our cleansing operation.
JUDGE. A word is planted in his brother's mouth
       A will is planted in his brother's mind.
THIRD BLACK PRISONER. We'll root the word out of
           his mouth
       And cut the will out of his mind.
JUDGE. A spectre rises from Petra's body
       A spectre crying that my justice
       Must die or fortify itself.
FOURTH BLACK PRISONER. That is the signal for our
           attack!
       When liberal justice whines of violence
       Power flies to those with the right of might.
JUDGE. Petra's murder
       Printed in a million newspapers
       Torn and carried by the wind,
       Tugs like entrails on the blackthorn
       And fouls the edges of the city
       Where greenness first begins.
FIRST BLACK PRISONER. Our martyrdom
       Blazoned on a million sheets of paper
       Is a trumpet blowing
       Millions to the cause
       Of heroes who warn the people's enemies

With this exemplary, just, horrible death.

JUDGE. Then, for the sake of such a peace
As still does mantle sunset villages
Where the heart may love and rest,
Which still to Europe I may restore;
And, for the survival of a vision
Within the human memory
Of absolute justice accepted by consent;
And for those margins of possibility
In our free actions, which open doors
To imagination and to music;
And, for the sake of my own integrity
Which drives me to an insupportable air
Where the earth, killed by tyrants,
Is cut away from under me——

SECOND BLACK PRISONER. Then, for the sake of an
indivisible nation
Embossed beneath one iron will;
And, for a conquering army led
To banish pity and thought;
And, for the purified blood like a tide
Streaming through heroic children;
And, to throw off our present chains,
With a gesture which is freedom
Proclaiming that our might is right——
We rise against your laws.

[*Threatening they rise up between the* JUDGE
*and the footlights, hiding him from the audi-
ence.*]

JUDGE [*retreating*]. My truth will win.

30

CHORUS OF BLACK PRISONERS. The people hear OUR
        voice.
    The people will change this sentence and make
        sentences
    Other than this.
                        CURTAIN

31

ACT II

ACT II

THE SMALL SCENE

[SCENE: *A room in the Palace of Justice. Bare and whitewashed with folding doors on right, leading through a passage directly to the Law Court. Another door, left. In front a window leading out onto the balcony. The* JUDGE'S WIFE, *a fat, masterly invalid of sixty, is talking to* HUMMELDORF, *a minister of the Government.* HUMMELDORF *is white-whiskered: he is in morning dress.*]

WIFE [*standing in front of the folding doors*]. No, no, I forbid you to see him. As his wife I put my foot down. A woman in my position doesn't expect any gratitude (I don't even ask my husband to waste one moment of his just, well-used time on me); but I can at least do my duty. How do you expect that justice would be CREATED in this Court if I wasn't here to protect my husband?

HUMMELDORF [*agitated*]. You must please believe me, I have come here on a very important matter. It is a question of whether the judge will agree to the reprieve of the prisoners who were condemned to death for the murder of a Polish Jew called Petra.

WIFE. Reprieve? Reprieve? When I've not been able to sleep for a week on account of the trouble these two cases have given my husband? Now that he's brought himself to condemn them, must he go through all that mental struggle again, a struggle which brought him to the very threshold of death, when offering these worthless creatures to their Maker, in order to fetch them back? No, Mr. Home Secretary, if you'd comforted that man, lying by his side night after night, you'd know that those who have made him suffer so much can NEVER be reprieved. The President of the State has his answer from ME: there will be NO reprieve.

HUMMELDORF. Of course the President of the State has the power to over-rule any decision, however exemplary, made by your husband. But, in this case, for the sake of the nation——

WIFE [*sitting down heavily in an armchair*]. Mr. Hummeldorf, if you have any consideration whatever, please don't TORTURE me with these requests any more. [*Drawing a rug over herself.*] As a matter of fact I'm an invalid and I simply haven't the strength. . . .

> [*The doors are thrown open, from within. The* JUDGE'S VOICE *is heard speaking, with intense feeling, from the Court.*]

JUDGE'S VOICE. But now, I say the change is rung
Whoever being a Judge
Errs from the centre of collected powers
Pointed into the State, is friend to murderers

And to that wandering outward fringe of rebel Disintegrators.

[*The* VOICE *is drowned in murmurs. Then there follows the noise of the Court dispersing.*]

WIFE [*to Hummeldorf*]. Please leave me. Allow me at least to have a few words with my husband alone.

HUMMELDORF. But, madam, I entreat you, there is a grave crisis. I must insist on speaking to your husband. Only he can now save the government——

WIFE. *I* shall arrange everything, Mr. Hummeldorf. My husband is an inspiring idealist but it is not he who makes decisions. How often in history does the last word of a great and splendid man lie with an unknown woman—his wife. And how little does history, written by men, recognise it! I shall call you in when I have spoken to my husband.

HUMMELDORF. Where shall I wait?

WIFE [*pointing to door on left*]. In there, in there.

[*Exit* HUMMELDORF, *left.*]

[*Enter* JUDGE.]

JUDGE. It is a judicial crime. The President of the State should reprieve them.

WIFE [*astonished*]. Who?

JUDGE. The three Communist prisoners whom I have just sentenced to death.

WIFE [*indignantly*]. Communists! And why should *they* be released, may I ask?

JUDGE [*pacing up and down*]. Because the sentence is unjust. Consider the whole situation. Since our country's defeat in the War, a new generation has

37

arisen. We, the older generation, secretly hoping that the young will regain what we lost, and conniving at a betrayal of the Treaty which we signed, have allowed these boys to acquire arms. Now, suddenly, a new law is passed, making it illegal to carry firearms: so that when a street fight takes place in which some of these young people are attacked by the Black Troops—or even by the police—I am asked to sentence them to the same death penalty as I passed on Petra's murderers. Yet this morning's case was a very different one from the planned bestiality of Petra's murder.

WIFE. I'm angry, really angry, that you bother about young people. What have they been since the War? Selfish, lazy, inconsiderate, self-indulgent, critical of those who are better and older than themselves. The best of the whole lot were killed in the War. Who cared then about the justice of millions of men being killed?

No, your heart did not break

When the world cracked

And our country's dear sons, like blood corpuscles,

Clotted to make a scar

Across the European gap.

JUDGE [*gently*]. Remember the mothers and fathers of these three young men.

WIFE. O, I'm glad, I'm glad I had no children. I hate this younger generation who are discontented, too lazy to work, ungrateful to those who slave day and night for them. They have no respect, reverence

nor decency. I wish that there would be another
war, like a great bonfire on which to cast these
faggots.

JUDGE. We teach our children killing. When their
    Generosity—bred in tender valleys
    Unplundered by the latest robber barons—
    Rises against lessons of death, it speaks
    Through mouths of revolvers which we taught.
    Then, still to maintain the gentlemanly cycle
    Of smiling disaster, we execute
    Their spiritual will armed against war.

WIFE. No, I am on the side of MEN who are still willing
to die for their country. The children of my
thoughts are those brave young men who murdered
Petra; they were patriots; they were willing to lose
their lives in order to rid the country of a RAT.

JUDGE. *My* children would live and die for a world in
which such acts of brutality were impossible.

WIFE [*bitterly*]. Then your children killed my children
in the womb. We are childless.

JUDGE. We can each fight for the lives of those who
might have been our children.

WIFE [*rising from her chair*]. Then I shall fight for the
lives of Petra's murderers. They are *my* children.
And I'll show whose side I am on. [*She walks over
to the door and opens it.*] Mr. Hummeldorf, my
husband will be glad to see you.

               [*Enter* HUMMELDORF.]

JUDGE. The Home Secretary—Mr. Hummeldorf! To
what do I owe this honour?

39

HUMMELDORF [*pompously, to* JUDGE]. I have come to
deliver a message of appreciation to you from the
President of the State, in recognition of the truly
awe-inspiring warning which you delivered yesterday to the armed Black bands. The President, in
his own words, appreciates in your speech almost
an excess of impartiality.

JUDGE. Well?

HUMMELDORF [*turning away and then producing press
cuttings from his coat pocket*]. You know, sir, that
the patriot leader has sent a telegram to the President of the State protesting against your sentence
on Petra's murderers?

JUDGE. No, no, he cannot be so foolish as to identify
himself with that outrage.

HUMMELDORF [*showing cuttings*]. You have seen these
cuttings?

JUDGE. They defile us! They hang upon the edges of
the city like fragments of Petra's entrails!

WIFE. What do the cuttings say?

HUMMELDORF. They say that your husband is a communist sympathiser.

WIFE [*to* JUDGE]. Monstrous! And you accept that!
You don't protest! You don't sue them! You don't
publicly denounce them!

JUDGE [*quietly*]. My truth will win.

HUMMELDORF. You don't realise the extent of this kind
of propaganda. At the moment the life of the government is endangered. Protest meetings are being held
all over the country. [*Walking across to the windows*

and looking out.] I shouldn't be surprised if the
Black Troops march on the Law Courts. [*Turning
back.*] In your position, you are able to discriminate when you pass judgments. That is the most
effective reply to the charge that you are a Red.

JUDGE. Ministers, lawyers, politicians, bishops,
All of you discriminate.
The murderer may go free, if he murders
The named enemies of your political system.
But if the passionate revolutionary
Grows violent through hunger or impatience,
The letters of the law are bars
Pulled down upon him when he slightly trips.
Listen!
Ten days ago, three young men were standing in the
great square opposite the railway station, handing
out communist leaflets, underneath the statue of a
poet who stares across the square at the trains de-
parting for the south. A police van stopped in front
of them, policemen leapt out and attacked them
with truncheons. You know, Mr. Hummeldorf, far
better than I do which side the police favour; I, as a
judge, have to reach conclusions offered by the well-
co-ordinated evidence of your police. Two of the
Communists attempted to run away, whilst the
third, covering their flight with a revolver, fired
several shots. One of them wounded a policeman in
the arm. Because not merely political violence but
even the carrying of firearms is a crime now made
punishable with death, I have condemned them all

41

to the same death as Petra's butchers. Well, well, I am prepared to interpret the law as I have done this morning and yesterday, but there is another law which speaks to my own conscience.

HUMMELDORF. You seem to forget that the law is intended to protect the State from enemies and not to fulfil an abstract ideal of justice.

JUDGE. Do you believe that these three young men deserve the same punishment as a gang of terroristic murderers?

HUMMELDORF [*furiously*]. Arguments! Arguments!
Here you sit fidgeting
At jig-saw patterns in this white, square room
When, outside, all the world in crisis
Shoots up to a prodigious firework.
Sir, fanciful as it seems, it is we
Who must shoulder responsibility—
Build huts against the blizzard from America,
Conduct defensive campaigns, should they prove
    necessary,
And put our shaken nation's house in order.
What are the lives of these three Communists?
Puff! Though they be innocent today, remember
Their creed draws them along a track of time
Leading to bloody murder tomorrow.
Why wait till then? Why not punish them
For your own death before they kill you?
We fought our enemies during five years,
Whole towns we bombed were innocent;
Yet now we are so scrupulous, we let

Our declared murderers grow in our midst
Lisping propaganda through revolvers.
Abstract justice is nonsense. This is war.
So kill, kill, kill.

WIFE. I agree with you absolutely, Herr Hummeldorf.

> [HUMMELDORF *goes over stage and clasps her warmly by the hand. Still holding her hand, he turns to the* JUDGE.]

HUMMELDORF. Sir, I have come to ask if you will retract the death sentence passed on Petra's murderers.

JUDGE. Then, through you, I submit to the President of the State that he should reprieve the three Communists whom I sentenced to death this morning.

HUMMELDORF. Even if I delivered that message, the President would be powerless. You don't seem to appreciate the situation. The Black Leader has thrown his whole movement into the support of Petra's murderers. If the government carry out the death sentences, *he* will come into power on a wave of public indignation. We have only one alternative: to reprieve the Black Prisoners and, at the same time to take the Black Leader, on certain conditions, into our government.

JUDGE. Then you will give power to a man who has identified himself with a horrible murder——

HUMMELDORF. We shall have him under our control. Otherwise, we must be ruled by him. . . . The President, of course, could reprieve Petra's murderers. But we wish, as far as possible, to keep him above politics. We therefore call upon you to withdraw publicly.

WIFE. But what a wonderful man this Black Leader must be, to be able to rise above his social position —he was the son of a coal-heaver, wasn't he?—and become a member of OUR government, so filled with his superiors!

HUMMELDORF [*elated and vulgar*]. Yes, madam,
The people united in a flooding sea
Of applauding waves waving handkerchiefs
Are behind successful Leaders who have landed
To receive power on the prosperous shore.
Any sacrifice is worth it.
Let considerations of party drop overboard
And with them all our abstract theories
And foreign logical principles.
I always say that we can waive all rules
So long as we still rule those waving waves!

JUDGE. First of all the President must reprieve the men I sentenced to death this morning.

HUMMELDORF. My dear Sir! You can talk like that! Reprieve the Communists! Let me tell you that, within a month, to be a communist will be an offence punishable with the executioner's axe. We have to make some sacrifices of opinion for the good of the whole country. [*Genuinely moved.*] My dear, kind, gentle, just, old schoolfellow, do you imagine that I would have agreed if I weren't convinced that this arrangement is absolutely necessary? I tell you, I have humbled myself these days.

44

I have been on my knees in the mud.

And, as a matter of fact, I am a proud man.

The Leader and his vulgar bodyguard

Laugh in my face and ape me behind my back.

I can see, though I am old; the old always see

That they are old, and the young, young.

They said my speeches were too long.

I was furious, and partly I could have wept

To see our world sink to its knees whilst theirs
arrived

With such insolence of mockery.

I'm old, I'm old.

WIFE. Yes, we're old, we're old. Outside these windows

Life has gone past us in a tidal wave

That swept the best away, depositing

On the pavement, only conceited, bubbling dregs.

JUDGE. When I resign, I shall state my reasons for
doing so. I shall publicly demand the death penalty
for Petra's murderers and the release of the three
Communists.

HUMMELDORF. Do you approve of the three Communists carrying revolvers?

JUDGE. No.

HUMMELDORF. Then will you appeal to their support-
ers, who also carry revolvers?

JUDGE. No.

HUMMELDORF. Then to whom will you appeal?

JUDGE. To the just.

HUMMELDORF. The just! Pooh! Allow me to tell you

that the just are those who will first be shot by one
side, and then, if there are any of them left, by the
other. And no one will care.

JUDGE. How strange it seems

That to me justice was once delineated by an inner
     eye
As sensibly as what is solid
In this room, tables, chairs and walls,
Is made indubitable by the sun.
But now all crumbles away
In coals of darkness, and the existence
Of what was black, white, evil, right
Becomes invisible, founders against us
Like lumber in a lightless garret.
I refresh myself in pleasant country
Or I stare round faces in a room
And although there is gold in the corn and gaiety
In a girl's eyes or sliding along the stream,
Everything is without a meaning.
Voices of hatred and of power
Call through my inner darkness
Only that might is right.

[HUMMELDORF *walks across to the windows and
throws them wide open. There is a murmur of
voices outside. During the rest of the act the
audience should feel that the actors within the
room have become slightly unreal; that the reality
is in the street outside.*]

HUMMELDORF. There is a crowd outside.
The breath grows from their mouths

Like waving flags of anger.

[*Cry from outside 'Release the Petra martyrs!'*]

JUDGE. So you have tried to force my hand?

HUMMELDORF. We have done nothing, nothing.

WIFE. For what is this the signal?

HUMMELDORF. It is the sign for a revolution

By those who are afraid of revolution—

A revolution of cowards

Who demand the rule of an iron hand

And the murder of the Reds

To save them from revolution.

WIFE. Do something quickly. Save us.

HUMMELDORF. All we need do is stay in power.

In particular, your husband can save us.

WIFE. How? How?

HUMMELDORF. By renouncing his sentence of death on Petra's murderers. By affirming that there is no question of reprieving the Communists. The rest we can do.

WIFE. Darling, save us!

HUMMELDORF. Understand that whether you go or stay, Petra's murderers will be released and the three Communists executed. If you stay, we may still save our honour.

WIFE. For the sake of matriarchy, for the sake of the barren and the unhappy who have moulded a whole strata of society into the altar of their enormous grievance, for the sake of those who claim the right to hate the sexual pleasures of young people, for the sake of the rich and the diseased, for the

47

sake of funerals, marriages in Church and the privileges of the laws of inheritance, for the sake of the past and the dead, O hear us!

HUMMELDORF. For the sake of the authority of fathers over their children, for the sake of the politicians of an older generation who are elected by the people for the purposes of concealing the real forces of competitive power, for the sake of the respectable and privileged survivors who adorn an age founded on vulgarity, for the sake of our schooldays, religion, the past and the dead—O hear us!

JUDGE. We are trampled beneath a brutal present
Far realer than our life-long dream
Where unrestrained new generations seemed
Always to move away as we drew near. But now
Their will grows over us making our appearances
Sham as the smiling grass on graves
Blown by the wind to belie death beneath.
Therefore, therefore my will lies
In a sleep from which the day wakes, and my voice
Which passed sentence on Petra's murderers,
Spoke in my heart locked beneath the turf
—Today denies it with a roaring gale.
I here bury my own will and cancel
My mystical hand and my unbiased sight.
I reprieve Petra's murderers and suffer those to die
Whom the time kills. Thus we who are ghosts
Survive amongst the new and potent living
To read by clearer and clearer signs
That day long past on which we died.

WIFE. I'm glad, I'm glad.

HUMMELDORF [*shaking hands with the* JUDGE]. Allow
me to congratulate you on your statesmanlike decision.

[*Shouts of the crowd outside 'Death! Death!'*]

WIFE [*transfigured*]. Why do they call out 'Death'?

Go out onto the balcony and let the people thank
you.

[JUDGE *goes out onto the balcony. His* WIFE *is
left alone, staring in front of her. Now, in addi-
tion to the murmur of the crowd outside, there is
a faint drum which grows louder and louder,
nearer and nearer as she speaks.*]

The drums beat. The flags are waving.
The men march down the street.
Everything has been wrong for forty years
Because I bore no child.
But now the decorated war restores
Men to their sun and women to their night.
The young will rise from each other's sleep,
The free to be disciplined, the happy to be killed.
My huge animal body was unsatisfied
My breasts were starved because they gave no food,
My cries of hatred were as instinctive
As the babe's scream till the nurse brings its nappy.
But now I forget my self-destroying poison :
In the larger hate which destroys the world
The time is redeemed and I am content.
Let the unconsidering compact bomb cut through
Tenements and the horizontal thoughts

Of civilization. It was all false, false,
Only my hatred and abrupt death were real.
Let all children be killed, their little dreams
Flake like ashes under the melted girders.
I have waited for this general anger
To lance my crippled soul of poison
Till my hate explodes in war like a bomb. I am
    glad.
Oh, love, I'm cured, I'm cured.

> [*Three loud taps of the drum as she throws off
> her shawl and rushes out onto the balcony to be
> received with an explosive burst of enthusiasm
> from the crowd while there falls the*
>
> CURTAIN.]

ACT III

ACT III

THE LARGE SCENE

[SCENE: *In front of the Palace of Justice. Railings, two trees, a street lamp, wide pavement, a raised speakers' rostrum, the shadowy building behind with faint lights in the first floor windows in front of which there is the balcony of the room in Act II.*]

[*Enter from one side* PETRA'S BROTHER, FIANCÉE *and* THIRD RED, *who is wounded: these form the* RED CHORUS. *From the other side enter the* BLACK CHORUS, *consisting of* SIXTH BLACK, SEVENTH BLACK *and a* BLACK TROOP LEADER, *dressed in officer's uniform, indistinguishable in type from the Prisoners in Act I, by whom they are joined later in this Act.*]

[*The two choruses remain at their respective sides of the stage, divided by the gap containing the speakers' rostrum and the balcony above; except when one or another speaker leaps forward excitedly onto the rostrum to make a longer speech.*]

[*Although no curtain falls during this Act, the*

53

*action is divided into separate scenes and these
divisions should be emphasised by pauses, different lighting, etc. The scene in which* PETRA'S
BROTHER *is shot recalls the atmosphere of Act I.*]

SIXTH BLACK. You here!

THIRD RED.   Again!

SIXTH BLACK.   I thought
    You'd been swabbed up resisting
    Our Petra blood bath.

FIANCÉE [*mocking*]. How feed your prisoned heroes?
            Your muscular five
    Heroes, who beat to death
    One coughing invalid? How are they paid?
    How do the bankers thank
    Their hired assassins?
    What office shall be given
    That liberal judge whose conscience will fret his
            hand
    To scratch pearly as pigeon on cold pavement
    Upon their paper sentence with his pardon?

THIRD RED. Yes, yes and who repairs
    The splayed heart of your Leader
    Who sits in the South and telegraphs his nerves
    Wired across the hundred headlines
    At one with Petra's butchers?

FIANCÉE. Who thanks? And who shall pay
    Statesmen who make a literal candle
    Of blazing parliaments?
    Dons whose learning heaps
    The living leaves of art upon a bonfire

54

In public squares under the eyes of statues,
Those lenses of the snow, through death's cold
    nothing
Staring at madness?

THIRD RED. Who pays, who pays
The doctors slick with instruments
And hiring out their minds
To castrate heritable intellect?
Whether precise with steel and frowning through
    pincenez
Or whether breeched in towering leather,
With the rhinoceros-hide whip crack
Or smiling castor oil, you are all the same.

BLACK TROOP LEADER. Take care. Take care.
Your doom hurries. Wait here an hour
And our engine will ride the track we've laid
Under which your bodies will be sleepers.
Death answers you with your own speechlessness.
In lightless cells, in spiritless caves of hunger,
Under insult of blows, your lives will seem
Never even to have existed.
We can build history. Moles will not
Tunnel your graves; nor swallows
Fly through your trackless questions.

SEVENTH BLACK. Bullets, not speeches
Answer such as you.

SIXTH BLACK. I unstrap my revolver
When I hear you speak of culture.

BLACK TROOP LEADER. Or be destroyed,
O elements of disunity, or enlist

In the army. Learn there
The inner peace of killing; touch bugle colours
Like golden ridges in the conscript's mind
Most hard and glittering at night
Under the moon and gusty flags
Which guard the deathly plain.

PETRA'S BROTHER [*leaping onto rostrum*]. Civilization
which was sweet
With love and words, after great wars
Terrifies; architraves
Or flowering leaf of the Corinthian capital
Momently threaten; then fall
In marble waves on life. What was
The fastened mouth of the clear past
Speaking in stone against the moving cloud, be-
comes
Our present death. Then those
Who still will live, must tear
The spiritual will from the material
Ruling pattern of rigid memory
And the system that haunts, to hew what's real
After the living thought, not think what the dead
have willed.
Fall marble, fall decay: but rise
Will to live, in brothers: build
Stones in the form of justice: not justice
Into the fall of funeral monuments.

BLACK CHORUS. Blasphemers against the Word!

RED CHORUS. Kneelers before dictators and the
sword!

BLACK CHORUS. You, who, after this life, will suffer
    eternal death.
RED CHORUS. This life, which you would turn to
    death!
BLACK CHORUS. We gain life after death.
RED CHORUS. You make death in life.
BLACK CHORUS. DEATH!
RED CHORUS. DEATH! [*Leader of* BLACK CHORUS
    draws his revolver.]
        [*The* JUDGE *comes out onto the balcony.*]
JUDGE. Do not put away your revolvers.
    If you wish, shoot, I may not protest.
    For I come to announce not my own resignation
    But the resignation of the law.
    As for me, I still wear an invisible office
    And am invisible; my judgments and will
    Resist you no more than the surrounding air.
    When Petra's murderers heard their sentence
    They heard a ghost speak and my voice which said
        death
    Spoke not to theirs but from its own grave.
    Petra's murderers go free. The precedent
    Licenses their acts to flourish like a tree
    Spreading murder which grows branches
    Above that soil where the law is buried.
    I scrap their death sentence.
    Their release will follow immediately.
        [*He tears a paper to pieces.*]
SIXTH BLACK, SEVENTH BLACK, and TROOP LEADER.
    This is our greatest victory!

PETRA'S BROTHER. But were our comrades also
    freed?
JUDGE. The same accomplished fact
    As freed Petra's murderers, sealed your friends'
        death,
    And set a dam across my mouth
    Beyond which no Judgment may flow.
FIANCÉE. Petra's death was a crime
    Without parallel in our time.
    Yet his murderers go free, whilst for an incident
    In which our comrades slightly wounded one man
    You do not relent.
JUDGE. Not only your comrades, who will die,
    But yourselves, are now a common target
    Held up by the country's laws
    For your enemies to shoot at—
    Assured of nothing but applause
    When they score a bull's eye.
    The most I can do for you, I now do:
    I advise you to flee from here quickly.
THIRD RED. No, no your Lordship, we'll stay and
        shout our protest
    Until this injustice is reversed.
JUDGE. Very well. But I must go.
PETRA'S BROTHER. No stay and join our side.
    With you to lead us,
    We'll form the masses in their ranks behind you
    To free our comrades
    And bring to justice those who murdered Petra.
JUDGE [hesitates]. And when the army opposes us?

PETRA'S BROTHER. We shall kill all who oppose us.

JUDGE. Then, to atone for one injustice
    We create many injustices.

FIANCÉE. You have the power to choose.

JUDGE [*slowly*]. No.

FIANCÉE. You are the mask they wear
    Who commit injustices and condone murder.
    When their actions are most naked
    And their knife flashes in an unashamed moon,
    They assume your look of justice
    And like a parrot you say 'regret, regret'.

JUDGE. The true face which I wear
    You will see, you will see.

PETRA'S BROTHER. Now, under my eyes,
    Your face changes to that face
    Which is the face of Petra's murderers.
    You are responsible for my brother's death.

JUDGE. I have done no murder, and I have saved your
        lives,
    If you will accept them from me.

PETRA'S BROTHER. We refuse to fly; and what you
        have done

PETRA'S BROTHER, FIANCÉE and THIRD RED.
    You will see, you will see.

    [*Enter* JUDGE'S WIFE *onto balcony.*]

WIFE. 'Death,' 'death,' they cried.
    The sun, which lost our Empire, now does rise,
    And when it sets again
    It will set in another dawn
    Where it gilds Africa for us.

PETRA'S BROTHER. Justice and Liberty are now mortally injured!

WIFE. Darling, darling, I'm cured, I'm cured.
It is a miracle.
I was so ill, bed-ridden until
I heard the people cry out 'Death!'
The dear old days are back and everything will soon be altered
With soldiers marching down the street.
My people, you will fight again
Behind a disciplined nation
To regain
All that we've lost of land and ocean.

JUDGE. Dear, the night is turning cold,
I think we should go in.

WIFE. I won't do as I'm told!
These brave, brave boys are going to win.
I feel myself a girl again.

JUDGE. To whatever place I turn my sight,
I stare at my own weakness
Which brings down a Polar night
Groaning with more than winter-long distress.
These nightmare-calving fields of ice
Through black air challenge my eyes
Which can filter out no dawn
From a tired, deceiving brain.
It is time to go in.
I have worked for many hours.
Dear, come back into the house.
Lead on.

60

[*Exeunt, from the balcony,* JUDGE *and* JUDGE'S
WIFE. *The Five Prisoners of the First Act are
released and join the* BLACK CHORUS.]
[*The* BLACKS *approach the* REDS *threateningly,
who draw involuntarily to one side of the stage.*]

BLACK PRISONERS. We regain our liberty!

SIXTH BLACK, SEVENTH BLACK, and BLACK TROOP
    LEADER.
  Which is the signal of victory.
  The world with all its riches springs towards us!

BLACK PRISONERS. Idealistic walls fell before us!

SIXTH BLACK, SEVENTH BLACK, and BLACK TROOP
    LEADER.
  Our light floods the machinery of State power
  Now. The lever craves the hand of the Leader.

BLACK PRISONERS. Plunged, plunged in our prison
  cells of yesterday
  Is the indecisive and agitating hour.

FIRST BLACK PRISONER. The time of action strikes.
  Under the windows of this judge
  Let us establish the accomplished fact
  Of our right to kill Petra
  And again all such as Petra.

SECOND BLACK PRISONER. We affirm our victory now
  or lose!

THIRD BLACK PRISONER. Hurry, hurry, hurry,
  Whispers rise from the malarial swamps.
  Plotters meet in cellars. Our secret enemies
  Cross frontiers and join those who ring us round.
  Anger gains pressure like steam under a dome

Sleep slides away through greasy darkness
And makes the night of all our leaders
A prison where guards beat a drum.
Commit the irrevocable outrage quickly
And found religion on it.

FIRST BLACK PRISONER. Hurry, hurry, hurry,
Kill one of these, the bitch preferably,
Just as we smashed the Polish trash Petra.
Then call down judgment
From the stuffed brain of this judge, our tame
     partridge,
Who released us but holds back the Communists
For death tomorrow. His heart that broke
Once today, we'll crack under our fingers
Every morning, making it squeal
Approval to a law of murder.
Now shoot.

PETRA'S BROTHER [*jumping onto rostrum*]. Do not
dare touch any one of us. We have come here,
using our legal right of free assembly, to make our
protest against the savage death sentences passed
on our comrades. We have offered no provocation:
whoever attacks us, will be committing a criminal
assault. We are protected by the laws of the
democracy and by the police.

BLACK TROOP LEADER. Comrade, comrade, see how
Everything is altered.
We who did violence stand here free
And honoured, whilst your companions perish.
The example of Petra's corpse

62

Shot and beaten with rods, is shown
Not as an exhibition of shame
But as what the law approves. Gunmen and gangsters
Are set free, whilst bars and manacles
Exist to guard them from their critics.

PETRA'S BROTHER. Then, standing under his windows,
We appeal directly to the Judge.

THIRD RED. Yes, we appeal to the Judge. He loves
true justice but his office is bound in the same
chains as bind our lives. When he understands this
—as he must now—he will be on our side.

[*The* JUDGE *appears in the window behind the
balcony. He is not seen by the Choruses.*]

FIANCÉE. He said that he had done no murder. He
offered us our lives which you would now take away.

THIRD RED. We call upon him that, later, he may call
upon us to establish true justice for the people,
founded on the strength of the people.

PETRA'S BROTHER [*ecstatic*]. The mountain streams
that have electric roots
The stones
And metals, all of them our plant;
We'll tear from where they stick in lives
Now their possessors; give them as a prize
To those who've worked in fields and factories
For many centuries.

THIRD RED. We shall form a united front with the
Judge to punish the enslavers and murderers of the
people and to reprieve those who are the people's
true representatives.

PETRA'S BROTHER [*ecstatic*]. Into the image of a heart
That feeds separate functions with blood they need
For what they make, we'll shape the wealth
Of the dispossessed world and let those riches pour
Their fertilising river delta
Across the starved sand of the peoples.

SIXTH BLACK. Your Judge has no power! His law is
founded on weakness. His rulings are not backed by
armies.

FIANCÉE. He still has the police with whom to keep
gangsters in order.

FIFTH BLACK PRISONER. Oh! Oh! The police are
on *our* side. Power calls to power and answers.

FOURTH BLACK PRISONER. Even the Judge secretly
supports us. We can save him from your revolution!
[*The* JUDGE *opens the French windows, but
does not go onto the balcony. The Choruses see
him.*]

PETRA'S BROTHER, FIANCÉE and THIRD RED
[*severally*]. Your Lordship! Your Lordship! Petra's
murderers threaten to assassinate us in the square.
Protect our legal right of free assembly! Unite with
us to establish free speech and democratic law!
Justify your impartiality!
[*The* JUDGE *goes back into the room and is not
seen.*]

BLACK CHORUS [*mocking*]. SILENCE!
SILENCE!
SILENCE!
Now we unstrap our revolvers.

64

RED CHORUS. Kneelers before dictators and the
    sword!
BLACK CHORUS. After this life, you shall suffer eter-
    nal death!
RED CHORUS. This life, which you now turn to death!
BLACK CHORUS. We gain life after death!
RED CHORUS. Your life is our death!
BLACK CHORUS. DEATH.
RED CHORUS. DEATH.

> [BLACK CHORUS *fire*. PETRA'S BROTHER
> *falls. Half-lights of illusion and uncertainty, re-*
> *calling the First Act.*]

PETRA'S BROTHER. I am wounded.
FIANCÉE [*runs to his side*]. Where are you hurt?
PETRA'S BROTHER. Here in my chest. It seems
    That like Petra, my brother, my last thoughts rise
    From blood-corrupted lungs.
    The lungs are weeds which wrap around our hearts,
    And if our hearts have pity, today they bleed.
FIANCÉE. Stay with me and be happy.
PETRA'S BROTHER. Do not say
    I was unhappy. I built my mind
    In the foundation of that world
    Which grows against chaos and will be happiness.
    My mind's own peace and my material interest
    Centred in a philosophy of unfearing crystal
    Whose radius is the peace of cities, and brilliance
    Lack of jealousy between men.
THIRD RED. Petra, you and your brother die as heroes.
PETRA'S BROTHER. Is the eye heroic,

E   65

Lying soft in the face as reed-fringed pool,
Because for perceiving it looks to light
And rejects shadowy obstacles
And cuts through night like a diamond to the moon
And has patience to stare a million years
Back to the sun clocked in primitive time?
Or is the mind heroic
Being boxed all life in prisoning skulls,
Lurking like a spy remote in the brain beyond dis-
    section,
Because it has travelled further North than explorers
And does not freeze in interstellar space?
Eye sees what it sees, the mind
Knows what it must know.
Do not say I was a hero.
I used simply my eyes, I perceived
With my mind, my deeds sprang
From the sensible will.

FIANCÉE. But we snatched love——

PETRA'S BROTHER. From death——

FIANCÉE. Between death and life
    Our love shall create a link——

PETRA'S BROTHER. Yes, curled in your body, my
    brother's child.

FIANCÉE. We'll tear love——

PETRA'S BROTHER. From the iron assertions of the
    time——

FIANCÉE. Between the slogans of comrades——

PETRA'S BROTHER. After the ten hours' day in the
    factory——

FIANCÉE. We forced love——
PETRA'S BROTHER. To grow in improbable places——
FIANCÉE. Under the street doorways——
PETRA'S BROTHER. The yawning railway arches——
FIANCÉE. One night of release in the park——
PETRA'S BROTHER. Under the trees blossoming with
    electric flowers——
FIANCÉE and PETRA'S BROTHER.
    Petra's child will be fruit of our will.
PETRA'S BROTHER. As the helmeted airman regards
    Through the glazed focus of height
    The bistre silent city abandoned like a leaf
    With veins in microscopic detail beneath him,
    So from my towered pause of death,
    O sweet carrier of life, my riveted eye looks
    Thirty years forward when your child is grown.
    Imagine if the children of this hour
    Grew free of the treelike shadows of their parents
    Falling across them with the fate of envy
    And with roots of greed that clutch their hearts.
    O leaves in sunlight, O more fortunate houses,
    O faces in the street, O lights . . . I die. . . [dies].
FIANCÉE. O, my dear love!
SIXTH BLACK [from the darkness].
    Now kill the others and say
    These were all shot when escaping from us.
FIANCÉE [rising from PETRA'S BROTHER'S side].
    Stop! Stop!
                    [They stand back, silenced.]
    When Petra slept with me,

I held the whole of life, but now that earth
With all its trees and lakes has turned away its side
And I am left in a cold space
Which is drained entirely of the two I love.
How can I work with friends or shoot my enemies,
Since if I measure population
Against these brothers, though they're dead, they
      live for me
More than the world and all survivors?
Your clever bullets which streamed through him
Put out the universe where it hung in his mind
And future time; for me who stay
Its comet lays waste forest tracks of meaning.
No remote caverns, untrodden spheres, delayed
Epochs, hold him where the heel may quicken
And our souls meet in music.
Throw down your revolvers. Your violence runs
Along rigid lines to destroy each other.
All we need is love. And yet we play
The meaningless game of a machine
Running in grooves laid down by death.
Go home and let me cry.

> [*A low drum. Enter* PETRA'S MOTHER. *She
> stands above* FIANCÉE *who leans over the body
> of* PETRA'S BROTHER. *Spotlight on her and*
> FIANCÉE. *The rest of the stage in darkness
> through which loom the silent figures of the*
> BLACK CHORUS.*]

MOTHER. Beloved sons,
      You start on that difficult journey

68

Away from light and towards the light
Where the black, plumed cypress burns invisibly.
You are forgotten and remembered
When Spring the tiger
Breaks the bones with clawing roots
And the worm of oblivion your flesh eats.
But between the cypresses
The roads lead to my heart,
You are born again in the womb
Where love remembers.

FIANCÉE. Terrible woman, I do not know you.

> [*Enter* JUDGE'S WIFE *who stands beside the*
> MOTHER, *over the* FIANCÉE.]

WIFE. My husband has not slept five nights.
He sleeps now. I shall not
Wake him for anyone. You are an inconsiderate,
Hard, selfish generation. I am very glad
That, when you feel at all, you are unhappy.
The younger Petra's killed; that's good:
Someone at last is taking measures.
You need not think I am shocked;
I am not afraid of corpses, having nursed
Our brave soldiers in the War.
They were more grateful than any of you, but they
        died.
Get up, foolish girl. Don't ask my pity.
You have never been through the brazier of love.
You only miss a physical enjoyment
Then cry like a child for a little painted doll.
And you, old woman, why should I give you money

Because your sons are dead? They were both
    scoundrels.
I do not ask for pity though I've never had
A son; and for that I could weep.

MOTHER. Beloved sons,
    When my love too at last forgets
    And the spirit attains earth's total night
    Then death is complete,
    The body forgiven
    The soul born again;
    God remembers
    Those whom the world forgets,
    And then the dawn of life breaks.

WIFE [*to* FIANCÉE]. I think I hate you more even than
    I hated
    That man who, being dead, you will not marry.
    At the end of his road there was a bullet!
    Of yours, yourself weeping with self-pity.
    I think men are fools to spare women
    Who, when they hold opinions, are the worst.
    If someone here should kill you, I have heard
    And shall see nothing.

                                    [*Exit.*]

MOTHER. Pity me that my second son
    Has gone to join the older one,
    I have no young strength to lean on.
    If for age you have any pity
    Of your charity throw me a little money.

            [*Exit* MOTHER. *Enter* JUDGE, *from below.*]

JUDGE. I have seen everything. I saw

This Petra murdered and I looked
Back into that brutal night now past
Where the elder Petra lies: and then as if
Those who were indeed poor in fact had funerals
I saw my own weakness as a hinge
On which the law turned to seal their deaths.
My mind no more dwells in printed codes
Ordered to peaceful judgments like a poem,
But in a cold dark vault, under a court
Where justice is murdered: and in cells
I see the trampled bodies of the dead
And hear the living shriek: and those
Who are the most disfigured, I yet recognize
As the most just: and from this vault
Run corridors through tall perspectives
Of future years until they break their shafts
Into a gaseous air amongst the scalding ruins
Of cities. Oh but
Everything will be changed—now I retract
The reprieve of Petra's murderers,
And I order the arrest of those who shot
Petra's brother here; and those
Three communists who were unjustly sentenced
My Court will try again.

    [HUMMELDORF *and the* JUDGE'S WIFE *appear
on the balcony. The* JUDGE *standing on the raised
pavement in the centre of the stage, with the balcony above him, and the* CHORUSES *below on
either side, is, as it were, at the centre of a
wheel.*]

HUMMELDORF. Sir, your resignation is accepted.
    I myself, as Minister of Justice
    In the National Government, have the painful duty
    Of telling you that you are superseded
    And that now you exceed your authority.

WIFE. Your wise and considered retraction of yesterday
    Is the foundation stone of our coalition.
    For that we are grateful and you will receive
        recognition.

HUMMELDORF. Yet we are very sorry
    To note that your unstatesmanlike liberal vice
    Of wavering at the moment of decision
    Has led to a distortion of your vision.

WIFE. There are a few of us
    Who, when the nation called, put on high office
    In the same spirit of pure self-sacrifice
    As the humblest private doffs his life for his country
        in the field.

HUMMELDORF. Of course, some voices will be raised
    To claim we acted from self-interest.
    Scoffers and grumblers are ever ready to
    Attribute the base motive not the nobler.
    That is the price we have to pay.

WIFE. But you have chosen an easier and more
        popular way.

JUDGE. Oh but that when
    These griefs that bite our hearts have come, they
        come
    Lacking all dignity. I am scampered over by rats,
    I mine no genuine vein of sorrow, my heart cracks

72

Alone and sterile because it is alone,
My thought has no general meaning,
My soul no root in this humanity;
Nor is there God or Satan to break
My final cry against. I envy, I envy
Those who had faith in the past to work the good
Or evil which they willed; who, when they died,
Had penetrated to the core of snow
Whose total freezing field their enemies invoked
To annihilate them. But we
Who are princes or ministers today, are only paint
On the town face of a commercial whore;
And if we are so mad as to imagine
That we control our offices, we learn
How we are nothing: our lives drop like mummies
Of the Egyptian past exposed to the real time.

FIANCÉE. Yes! Be like Christ!
Stand there, time's martyr, with your thin
Sexless body stripped, and the protruding ribs
Scarred on your side like weals of whips.
Let your self-pitying eyes sink
Deep into their bone wells and stare
At the world's tragedy played out in that one skull.
Let the iron outward spear
Knock at your heart in vain; your answer is the same
To those who kill you, as that you gave my lover
—Blood and water and death!

THIRD RED. For Christ also
With his great death betrayed
Humanity he might have saved.

73

FIANCÉE. Since when, his Church holds up a golden
    bowl
    In which the innocent fingers wash away
    The world's guilt from the purified soul.
JUDGE. I live and die in a vacuum
    Of misery without a name.
BLACK TROOP LEADER [*leaping forward with a flag*].
    Ring all the bells, hang out the flags,
    Amaze Europe with proclamatory acts
    Break through the streets like a waterfall
    Armies of men, destroying all
    Twigs and voices of opposition
    With insuperable derision.
        [BLACK CHORUS *close round the* JUDGE, *as
        at the end of the First Act.*]
CHORUS OF BLACK PRISONERS.
    The people hear our voice
    The people approve our sentences.
SECOND BLACK PRISONER. We demand our right
    That we should judge this judge
    By whom we were condemned.
HUMMELDORF. The people's justice is the servant
    Of the people's wishes;
    Take him away: and the others too.
BLACK TROOP LEADER [*from his prominent position
    now on the rostrum*]. The world we conquer must
    corrupt our souls.
    Its mineral veins will pour into our blood
    Making the will iron. Our language
    Will be the bomber's drum on the sky's skin.

74

The quickly conquered spaces
Will empty on our minds making them sterile
As deserts from which music is banished.
The population will be soldiers,
Innumerable, shifting and permanent in their vast-
    ness,
Terrific, like sands.

CHORUS OF BLACK PRISONERS. Till now all have
    feared power but we shall use it.

SIXTH BLACK, SEVENTH BLACK, and BLACK TROOP
    LEADER.

With terror and violence we shall abuse it.

    [*As the* JUDGE *and* REDS *are led away prison-
    ers, there falls the*
        CURTAIN.]

ACT IV

ACT IV

THE TRIAL

[SCENE: *The Curtain rises on three of the* BLACK
PRISONERS, *their arms linked together. They give the
impression of being hilariously tipsy. The stage is empty
in front, with benches rising in tiers behind. In the centre
(corresponding to the place of the speakers' rostrum in Act
III), there is a carved Judge's chair.*]

> [*Just as Act I is a dream in the Judge's mind,
> this act is Hummeldorf's dream.*]

THIRD BLACK PRISONER. Heads will roll. Blood must
flow.

FIRST BLACK PRISONER. Your Lordship, we find all
the prisoners guilty.

SECOND BLACK PRISONER. Discretion, my friend,
discretion. You and I, who are in the confidence of
the government, we know they're guilty, but we
don't say so till we've tried them.

FIRST BLACK PRISONER. Steady, steady, steady. In
my opinion, that's a very tendentious thing to
say ... the sort of bastard impartial thing a Jew
might say. Guilty! Of course they're guilty! Apply

philosophy to the question. Point One: *All other races are inferior, qualitatively, biologically and metaphysically to our stock.*

THIRD BLACK PRISONER [*monotonously*]. Blood must flow. Blood must flow.

FIRST BLACK PRISONER [*continuing, in a lecturer's voice*]. Our Science, which differs from decadent, Jewish, international science, in being biologically scientific—Point Two—*on account of the racial purity of the scientific workers themselves*, tells us that we are descended directly from the Greek Gods, whereas *they* belong to another race of *objects*—nails, chairs, stones, *things*, that is to say.

THIRD BLACK PRISONER. Heads will roll.

SECOND BLACK PRISONER. Nails, chairs, stones, bitches, swine, objects, Jews, nothing. Blood will flow.

FIRST BLACK PRISONER. They're nothing, which is the same as to say—Point Three—*The Jews are whatever we think they are: they are just bad dreams in our own minds.* Without us, they don't exist: with us thinking so, they're all shadows plotting to kill us, whispering like birds in the branches of the trees. [*Becoming hysterical.*] Yes, kill the Jews, they suck our blood and defile our daughters. Kill the liberals, who make us ridiculous in the eyes of the world. Kill. Kill these shadows quickly, before they overwhelm us in their universal night of chaos. Kill them, like that [*taking a leather whip from his belt, he lunges at a shadow*]. You see, they don't

exist, the perfidious swine. *Truth is only relative*:
That's Point . . .—where am I? What did I say?

THIRD BLACK PRISONER. Blood must flow, I say.
Blood must flow.

FIRST BLACK PRISONER. Steady, steady, steady.
[*Suddenly becoming maternal, he pats* THIRD BLACK
PRISONER *on the shoulder*.] There, there, my man,
don't worry. Blood *will* flow. It's written in the
Party Programme.

SECOND BLACK PRISONER. Then what do we find the
Judge guilty of?

  [*They move to the front of the stage, becoming
  idealized, as in Act I.*]

FIRST BLACK PRISONER. Guilty of dishonouring the
cause of our heroic dead!
Honour War and blood of soldiers, wet-
gushing from the khaki plain, made flat
With four years of violence and of rain.
Weep for the betrayal of our blonde straight stem
Of heroic men,
By ringleted, dark, sly men,
Emigrants from the East and parasites
Who wear red, wave red flags and refuse to pour
their veins
Into our world-conquering sacrificial stream.

SECOND BLACK PRISONER. Stabbed in the back, our
warriors were betrayed
Since when, chains have bound us for many years
Of slavery worse than conquest: years of secret
despair

Tunnelled under feather lightness of the dance hall
and the bar.

THIRD BLACK PRISONER. Stare North, East, West,
and remember
Shame of our countryside, shame of our corn,
Confiscated territories, self-sunk battleships,
Gangrened corpses, colonists forced to foreign
allegiance,
Shame of vines, coal and iron exiled beyond our
borders
By the pernicious Peace Treaty signature.

FIRST BLACK PRISONER. Prairie dogs have ravished
our flesh and our bones
The sword has scattered, but O they will reassemble
Into a brittle and pitiless army
In death's hollow valley at the word of order.

[*Enter* HUMMELDORF *in the robes of the Judge.
He goes to the Judge's chair.*]

HUMMELDORF. Bring in the prisoners.

[JUDGE, FIANCÉE *and* THIRD RED *are
brought in, accompanied by* BLACK TROOP
LEADER, *the* JUDGE *with his hands tied to a
stake which is planted into the front of the stage.*
FIANCÉE *and* THIRD RED *are put behind the
Prisoners' Bar, which is near the benches.*]

HUMMELDORF. Regret. Let me remember. Regret.
I do regret a change made in the law,
Which, acting retrospectively, makes your crime
Punishable with death.

JUDGE. I wish to make a protest.

82

HUMMELDORF. Silence! You will not speak until you
   are called upon to do so. . . . I declare the session
   opened.
THIRD BLACK PRISONER. Let him speak! Give him
   enough rope to hang himself with!
HUMMELDORF. Silence!
SECOND BLACK PRISONER. Who are you, to say
   silence to us?
   We are the Judges
   Who sit upon the Bench to judge this Judge.
FIRST BLACK PRISONER. You're a mascot, a stuffed
   bird, old wind-bag.
   Mind how you behave, and obey our orders.
HUMMELDORF. I have come to interpret the new law
   Which was made, I think, to press the State
   Back to the true source of its power
   Which is the strength of those who hold power,
   Expressed in the will of a Leader
   To build an army and establish order.
   My patriotism is so sincere
   That, for my country, I have come to sacrifice
   This man—my friend—whose only weakness
   Was his faith in an absolute justice
   Beyond the State and beyond the law,
   Existing in the balance of his own eyes
   Without the compulsion of the police.
   Now let the individual fail
   And the State have revenge
   And order build its army.
THIRD BLACK PRISONER. Then watch well the fate
                        83

of this other Judge, who interpreted his conscience
too faithfully.

FIRST BLACK PRISONER. You are brought here to
see what happens to Judges who forget that they
are the servants of the national will.

SECOND BLACK PRISONER. This was the old fool who
said that our Leader would be in chains so long as
he himself remained in power.

HUMMELDORF. Gentlemen, gentlemen,
We are bound each to each by many chains
Of mutual interest, which bind me to you
As they bind you in the centre of your power.

FIRST BLACK PRISONER. Slave, slave, see who is in
chains now. Observe the whip [*producing whip*].
Obey, obey. Get on with the trial.

HUMMELDORF [*ingratiating*]. Certainly, gentlemen, I
am the instrument of the People's Justice. [*To
JUDGE.*] You may now make your protest.

JUDGE. I am tied to a stake
And honoured with the superstitious awe
They saved for witches in the Middle Ages.
At night my hands are chained together
My feet chained to a pillar
In a stone cell under the ground
Where I am brought only bread and water.
Meanwhile, the newspapers,
Which my ironic gaolers read me
Outline my criminal treachery, discovering
That my house is stuffed with bombs,
My attics equipped, I think, with aeroplanes

84

And that two battleships float like ducks
Upon a little pond in my garden.
It is my last luxury to laugh: and you,
Whoever wishes, may laugh also.
But the dumb people fed with lies
And living in crazed darkness accept
The least credible lie as the most true
Which mirrors on this night of day today
The repetition of that terror
Which is their waking life and world.

HUMMELDORF. Release him from his chains.

> [*The* JUDGE *is released. He steps to the front of
> the stage and addresses the audience.*]

JUDGE. I speak from the centre of a stage
Not of a tragedy but a farce
Where I am the spiritual unsmiling clown
Defeated by the brutal swearing giant
Whose law is power, his order
Nature's intolerant chaos;
Here my defeat shows bare its desert
In which emptiness wins and force levels
Wastes meaningless except to mockery.
Laugh if you will at the mind's and body's weak-
ness
Yet if you multiply my single death
By all the deaths for which it is one precedent,
You see in my fall the fall of cities,
In this my innocent injured protest,
The massacre of children; in the triumph
Of those who hold me here

85

Your history clamped in iron; your word ground
Beneath the oppression of an age of ice.

HUMMELDORF. What is the charge against this man?

> [*At this question the* BLACK TROOP LEADER
> *comes forward reassuringly; as he makes his
> speech, he strolls about the stage with the re-
> assuring gestures of a middle-class holiday
> maker, occasionally practising a golfing stroke,
> or casting nautical glances from an imaginary
> sea front; that is, except when, as the dialogue
> indicates, he momentarily forgets himself and
> becomes threatening.*]

BLACK TROOP LEADER. Before I say anything else,
I want to repudiate emphatically the suggestion
that there is anything sinister or alarming about
us. It is necessary to expose this insinuation in its
vile nakedness and state [*glaring round suspiciously*]
that we know there exist certain evil international
forces, directed mostly from abroad, which are
anxious to calumniate us, to undermine the simple
faith of the man in the street who never doubts us,
for the sake of whose child-like trust we are deter-
mined to root out these mockers and grumblers
with the utmost severity.

SECOND BLACK PRISONER. Nails, chairs, stones,
bitches, swine, objects, Jews, nothing.

BLACK TROOP LEADER. As a matter of fact, we're
ordinary, decent, bourgeois people—most of us
happily married and myself, I may add, the
proud father of six. Most of us own a little scrap of

86

harmless property, a small shop with a bell that tinkles happily to summon mother when you open the door, or an acre or so of land, perhaps even a vineyard with the soft tendrils of the grapes and the fine globular fruit clustering around the ripe cheeks of our laughing children and young wives. Our pleasures are in healthy exercise that breeds a fine race of manly soldiers, and in the use of our few proud possessions; in playing the piano or taking a brisk drive with all the family in the little four-seater. But we still have a pride—however little we reck of possessions—a pride in our standard of living, a pride in our little property, a pride in this nation which we dream of as our own.

THIRD BLACK PRISONER. Yes, and when our rights are challenged, we fight to kill. Heads roll, blood flows, that's it.

BLACK TROOP LEADER. We are the same stock as those who went forth to the War, many to give their life-blood for Caesar and country. Our Crusade is one with theirs. Yet this new enemy against whom we bear arms is worse, far worse than those olden chivalrous enemies of rival nationhood fought in many a battle by our fathers; for we fight dragons, decadence, monsters, an evil which threatens the very foundations of our civilization. We went forth: and lo, already we return as victors. At the first assault we have slain the dragon in our land. It remains only that like a knight-errant of old guarding the honour of some

distressed damsel, we go forth to save other
nations—if need be against their will—for the
common weal of civilization.

SECOND BLACK PRISONER. Blood must flow.

THIRD BLACK PRISONER. Now I'm telling you, if we
hadn't done what we done yesterday, you'd all of
you—sitting there now so safe and sound—have
been the victims of bloody revolution. Dead, the
whole lot of you. They were armed to the teeth,
every scrap of paper we tore off them scribbled
over with sinister messages written in invisible ink.
In the nick of time we saved the country from a
revolution.

[*The Red prisoners begin to laugh.*]

SECOND BLACK PRISONER. What are those swine
laughing at? [*To* HUMMELDORF.] Pass the Death
Sentence at once—I demand it, or you'll be shot
too. No. Wait. [*To Red Prisoners.*] Wait till we get
you out of this Court, you scum, dead or alive, it
will all be the same in twenty-four hours. Lamp
posts, sewers, knives, quick-lime.

[*They continue to laugh.*]

THIRD BLACK PRISONER [*hysterically*]. They don't
exist, they don't exist, the dirty swine. Kill these
shadows, kill these shadows quickly. [*He advances
towards them with his whip raised.*]

HUMMELDORF [*as if to himself*]. To establish my world
on stone
I grope for the foundations
On which the past was built

88

But they slide away like waters
Whose opened surface has uncovered
Voices of torment, faces of chaos,
The fall of the great house.
I begin to lose all patience . . .
Regret. Let me remember. Regret.

THIRD RED [*quietly to* THIRD BLACK PRISONER].
Comrade, with the night these shadows will only
grow longer.

BLACK TROOP LEADER. Stick to the procedure. It's
the Judge whom we must try.

THIRD BLACK PRISONER. Yes, the filthy Judge!

BLACK TROOP LEADER. A week ago this Judge, whose
origins, it is scarcely necessary to add, are Jewish,
had the opportunity of showing whether or no he
was a patriot. He had to try five self-elected soldiers
of their country who, in the interests of the glorious
national resurgence, had rid their country of a rat—
Petra. On the next day he tried three red inter-
nationalist scum who had shot a policeman, one
of our most trusted agents. True to his Jewish
origins and his international sympathies, whom did
he sentence to death?

THE THREE BLACK PRISONERS. US!

BLACK TROOP LEADER. And whom did he attempt
to release?

THE THREE BLACK PRISONERS. THEM! [*pointing to*
THIRD RED *and* FIANCÉE.]

BLACK TROOP LEADER. Of what crime does every indignant and decent patriot without fail find him guilty?

89

[*The Court rises, all except* HUMMELDORF, *who looks perturbed,* THIRD RED *and* FIANCÉE.]

ALL THOSE WHO ARE STANDING. TREASON!

HUMMELDORF [*rising*]. Please sit down. [*They do so.*]
 What has the prisoner to say?

JUDGE. That I am guilty.
 For by your law, the jungle
 Is established; and the tiger's safety is guaranteed
 When he hunts his innocent victim,
 By all the iron of the police.
 I condemned to death gunmen
 And gangsters, but they are
 The highest functions of this society;
 Except perhaps for machine guns and those in-
  human
 Instruments of killing
 Which are more powerful even than your fangs
 Devoid of pity and the human spirit—
 As indeed the time may show.
 Where death is esteemed so highly,
 Where death's administrators are the nation's
  ministers,
 Here in death's court, judged by death's slaves,
 I should be flattered to die: perhaps I am.
 You could scarcely offer a more glittering honour.
 I appeal to those
 Who have sent the ambassadors of their powers
 Into this room which well may be the tomb
 Of justice for us and them
 Not to conceal their horror

90

At the usurping of law by lawlessness
Itself made into law
To justify Petra's murder.
Let them speak as witnesses
That I am killed for nothing worse
Than my indignation against murderers,
My pity for those three who did no murder.
Let them note well my tragic error
Fatal to repeat
When I renounced my public anger
Before imagined expediency.
Then let them turn their faces to a future
Of solemn words broken by rule,
Of spiritual words burned up with libraries,
And the triumph of injustice;
Of tyrants who send their messages of terror
Against the civilized and helpless.
O let them witness
That my fate is the angel of their fate,
The angel of Europe,
And the spirit of Europe destroyed with my defeat.

THIRD BLACK PRISONER. Treason! Treason! He has
    appealed to foreign public opinion. Condemn the
    prisoners instantly.

HUMMELDORF. For God's sake, wait. [*Turning desper-
    ately to the* JUDGE, *as though for illumination.*]
    What have you still to say?

JUDGE. Sir, amongst the clamour and the weight
    Of this event which presses on the time
    Like years of roots and soil above our graves,

My guilt, yes, my guilt, only my guilt,
Remains a star and legible compass,
There to read the true responsibility.
There was a river in a sky of storm
Where had I plunged my hands and torn
The clouds apart, there now would be a joy
Of peace vast as the sky.
If when I saw that sign, if when I reached
That pole on which a generation turned and all that
    space
Of geography which is our country,
If then at least I had not betrayed myself,
These still unreal acts would be indeed a dream.
I was a traitor. That is true. Because
I might have made all of this otherwise.

BLACK TROOP LEADER. We demand not only that
    you sentence the prisoner to death but that his
    name be recorded as that of a traitor in the history
    books taught to the younger generation of this
    country.

HUMMELDORF [*trembling and excited*]. No. No. This is
    monstrous. I protest.
Take his life, which he will gladly give.
And take mine too: let it lie down with his.
But when his soul has found release
From the mad torments of your living Hell
You may not smear it with your finger-prints.
No. Let it go alone to face
The terrible examining instruments
Of God, or history . . .

Oh kind, gentle, just, man,
How I remember now our youth together
And its promises, all betrayed.
Forgive me. Please forgive me.

JUDGE. Herr Hummeldorf, we each of us stand greatly
in need of forgiveness, though not from each other,
from those unborn generations.

HUMMELDORF [*to Judge*]. O Sir, I follow
Where you have gone. [*To Court.*] Now I retract
All that I said to condemn this man.
His example leads me into a cave,
Dripping with blood, where the two Petras lie
Dead in each other's arms; their horrible deaths
Are light and healing after this Court,
Since truth sweats through their agony, and mercy
At their tomb entrance lights a dawn
Which pleads for those three others
Who were most unjustly sentenced.

> [*Walking blindly forward*, HUMMELDORF, *with
> the lights on him, enters a world of illusions and
> uncertainty, where the* CHORUS *seem shadows.*]

FIRST, SECOND and THIRD BLACK PRISONERS
[*surrounding* HUMMELDORF *as they surrounded the*
JUDGE *at the end of Act I*].
The people hear our voice
The people have changed this sentence and make
sentences
Other than this.

HUMMELDORF. The corpse of Petra is a witness
His wounds are mouths speaking red words.

93

FIRST BLACK PRISONER. The life of Petra was an ulcer
    We cut out of our country's body.

HUMMELDORF. A word was planted in his brother's
    mouth
    A will was planted in his brother's mind.

SECOND BLACK PRISONER. We tore the word out of
    his mouth
    And cut the will out of his mind.

HUMMELDORF. A spectre rises from Petra's body
    A spectre crying that my justice
    Must die or fortify itself.

BLACK TROOP LEADER [*leaping forward*]. Shadows,
    shadows, surrounding us. Kill these shadows
    quickly.
    Trust no one. [*He strikes* HUMMELDORF *with his
    whip.*]

SECOND BLACK PRISONER. Seize Hummeldorf.
    [*Enter the other two* BLACK PRISONERS, *who do so.*]
    Send him to the cells at once. Let no one hear or
    speak of him. Dispose of the Judge and the other
    prisoners.

THIRD BLACK PRISONER. Announce that he is mad.
    Unfortunately the session is interrupted by his
    having a fit. Destroy all photographs taken and all
    reports of speeches in this Court. The last ten
    minutes are wiped out. *They never happened.*

BLACK TROOP LEADER [*advancing to the front of the
    stage*]. If your imaginations
    Invent and publish any picture of this scene,
    Remember that the lines cut by memory

Into the brain may cut so deep
They kill life altogether.
Delete those lines. Make your brains blank. Or——
You have seen and heard nothing
Except the fate of those who are traitors. [*Calling behind the stage.*] Ring down the curtain.

CURTAIN

ACT V

ACT V

THE THREE CELLS

[*The stage is separated into three cells. One, to the left is a yard, containing a tree. The second, in the middle, is a prison cell, bare, white and simply furnished. The third, to the right, is a Guard Room.*]

[*The* JUDGE, THIRD RED *and* FIANCÉE *are seated in the centre cell, talking quietly. They are dressed in prison uniform.*]

JUDGE. And ... And ... And ...

And released the Communist prisoners . . . And resigned

When the aged President demanded the retraction ...

And if I had published the statement of my reasons ...

For all Liberals of goodwill to consider ...

And if then ...

THIRD RED. No, no, you are neither so wrong

Nor so responsible as you would like to be.

Had you obstructed those loyal colleagues
Hummeldorf and your angry wife,
They would have swept you aside and published
Their explanations which, not being exactly libel-
lous,
Would yet suggest that, except for the law of libel,
Which notoriously outlaws truth,
And except for their recognition of your former ser-
vices,
Truths might come out which are better kept
quiet—
At worst that you yourself were that still unnamed
crisis
Against which their National Government was
formed:
At best, that you are insane and need a rest.

JUDGE [*smiling*]. That I am mad is perhaps true
For the truth I see is truth, or was: and perhaps
truth
As it exists in me, is mad. For what is madness
Except one's sense of final reality
Which has become an exile from his world
And from his time?

FIANCÉE. No, no, you are not that mad and glittering
snowman
Which you imagine. Simply, you are mistaken.
It is your misfortune, for which we pity you,
That being too honest for one time, you lacked
strength
To be born into another.

100

THIRD RED. Your tragedy
> Is not a Beethoven symphony where the hidden
> > silence
> Of the deaf genius becomes the terrible core
> Of all his sound, and symbol
> Of suffering humanity.
> There is no suffering humanity
> In whom your death will be the multifoliate rose
> Of a Christian sunrise
> Speared on the eternal mountain snows.
> There are no weak and meek whom you must pity
> Merging in them your own identity;
> As for the oppressed, they will be the strong,
> Not to weep over but make weep
> Those who are now their oppressors.

FIANCÉE. Our heroes—for example, my lover and his
> > brother—
> Are not the seven-pointed indrawn stars
> The centres of their crepe and tear-stained skies,
> But those for whom a freed humanity
> Was their joint aim, their lives
> Spent like two bullets
> To hit that single target.

JUDGE. Dear friend, your world is the antipodes
> Of the world of those
> Who seal us in this living tomb:
> And travelling there, where all seems opposite,
> Yet all will be the same; only
> Those who are now oppressed will be the oppressors,
> The oppressors the oppressed. For your

World and theirs exist to maintain their worlds
And truth becomes the slave of the arrangements
Whilst abstract reasoning is treated as a traitor
Sniped at by necessity.

FIANCÉE. Your world, comrade, is built upon a lie
Which is the suffering of many that the enlightened
    few
May pick truths out of chaos
Then claim 'beauty is truth, truth beauty' to
    justify
The injustice of the total lie
By saying it pressed those diamonds
From years of dark and terror.

THIRD RED. But our world is built upon
The freedom of the peoples, when
Those who dig the minerals for their own fetters
And build the implacable aeroplanes
The enemy aeroplanes which terribly,
Ignominiously, clutch their children;
Those who are common as the chafing seas
Equal in having nothing throughout the world,
With no nation except their poverty
And their manifold exploited powers—
Will use the mountainous strength of their own arms
Which now pile down against them, to dispossess
Their destructive few oppressors.
Winning is our reality; that once gained
Then freedom will push leaves from victory
And in the borderless world of the many
States and separate power melt away.

102

But you in fighting these our enemies
Who kill you to delete your words,
Yet see with their hypocrite mind; you disclaim
The necessary killing hatred,
And ignore that you or they must die.
You accept gentility, plead for their approval,
Even in death you sign the martyrs' truce
Of christians who have let themselves be killed,
Clasping the lovely flowering crown and white
Innocence of a saint's winding sheet;
You exchange your life for your murderer's bouquet
And murder your own will to earn his honour.

JUDGE. Yet I believe
That if we reject the violence
Which they use, we coil
At least within ourselves, that life
Which grows at last into a world.
Then, from the impregnable centre
Of what we are, we answer
Their injustice with justice, their running
Terroristic lie with fixed truth.
Our single and simple being
Will be the terrible angel
And white witness which though they deny
Betrays even their convoluted darkness.
But if we use their methods
Of lies and hate, then we betray
The achievement in ourselves; our truth
Becomes the prisoner of necessity
Equally with their untruth, ourselves

Their stone and stupid opposite.
And I believe
That in our acts we are responsible
Before a final judgment, whether indeed
Those legends of belief which made
The traditional sky fluid with prayer
Freeze time suddenly into a single crystal
Where history is transparent; or whether
Each generation is the outpost
Of a total spiritual territory
And defeats, even of necessity,
Are defeats indeed: for they transmit
The violence and hatred which we used
And the children's faces which we breed
Grow into those enemy faces
We gave our lives to kill.

> [*Enter, to the left, in the yard, a* JEWISH PRISONER *followed by one of the* BLACK CHORUS *with a whip, who orders him by signs. Fatly and heavily he climbs into the tree.*]

FIANCÉE and THIRD RED. Look there!

JEWISH PRISONER [*sings grotesquely*]. In the land of
bears and Arctic breezes
Cock o' the North all the ice unfreezes,
With his wooden pole he quickly unpegs
The Esquimaux belles, Minx, Skate and Megs.

JUDGE. Who are you?

JEWISH PRISONER [*sings grotesquely*]. Though he
hasn't succeeded in thawing me
Sighed the body strung on the gallows tree.

104

JUDGE. Why are you sent here?

JEWISH PRISONER [*whispering*]. I am sent to make you
mad.

FIANCÉE. Who are you? ... Who *were* you?

JEWISH PRISONER [*still whispering*]. I was a Jewish
doctor in Breslau.

I had a clinic for women's diseases.

THIRD RED. What have those filthy scum done to
you?

JEWISH PRISONER [*falling heavily from tree, shouts*].
They have robbed me of consciousness!
They have robbed me of consciousness!
[*Whimpering.*] They are coming to take me away.
They are coming to take me away. [*He faints.*]
> [*Enter two more of Black Guard to take him
> away; whilst they do so, from a cell behind the
> stage is heard*]

A VOICE. . . . And ye that have sinned, ye Black
Guardsmen and ye soldiers, ye that strike the innocent down, remember that the Day of Judgment
will come for ye also. . . .
> [*Interruptions of hoarse laughter.*]
For the Lord seeth all things. . . . You must not
arrest anyone. . . . You must be good or you will be
punished. . . . O believe my words when I preach
unto ye, for I am Jesus Christ the Son of God.[1]

THIRD RED. And those are the voices of the world we
leave:

The feathered isolation in the city

[1] This incident is quoted from *I Was Hitler's Prisoner*, by Stefan Lorant.

Of the adventure to love. Voice
Of the cheap preacher on the cheap box in the
    park
Furred also with sin's luxury.

JUDGE. Yet here in peace I can at last accept
My own unnameable shortcomings, tied
Into a moral sack, like the dumbed clapper
Of a cathedral bell, for thirty years.
I was unhappy and I did not know it.
I did not love my wife and I did not know it.
My misery and hatred
Left my wife childless, and hatred
Was the one rich fruit of her life.

FIANCÉE. I think, I think ...

JUDGE [gently]. What do you think?

FIANCÉE. I think that when my lover died, his life
Was planted in my sleep so when I wake
To the gusty day, it is as though I had returned
From the desirable earth, whose roots
Still wrap about me, to a luminous cold death.

JUDGE. Poor child, your heart is locked
Within that cold and withering vice
Beneath the ground, which was Petra's heart.

THIRD RED. What do you think? Waiting here
For death, what do you think?

JUDGE. The agony breaks through my veins
Which blaze till all my being
Has blossomed in a single flower of fire
Where I am at the centre of the sky.
Everything is life and is good.

For example, Christ the brother of Hercules, with
     childish hands
Snaps the twin serpents, which are warring nations;
For example, Christ is Apollo and makes men
     transparent
Seen through by his merciless disk of light.
And through all these days
I think often of that powerful man
Henry the Emperor at Canossa
Who waited four days in the snow, until the grace
Of the Pope melted nature's fixed whiteness
Into such blessed forgiving as the soul drinks.
THIRD RED. You are wrong, wrong. We are nothing.
     We have fallen
Into the dark and shall be destroyed.
Think though, that in this darkness
We hold the secret hub of an idea
Whose living sunlit wheel revolves in future years
     outside.
As for our lives
When they are killed they fall like seeds
Into the ground to bear the tenfold fruit
Of our purpose; thirty spring up,
O, all the statistics show, where three comrades
     die.
But we ourselves are husks. Honour
Is not buried with us, nor projected
On the horizon to write our names
Through that blazing instant when the squad shoots.
No, honour forgets

Our minds, rejects our bodies, rises
In other bodies and wears better days.
JUDGE.
[*During this speech a drum taps, louder and louder.*]
Always through my life I heard
Behind the music of the summer hills
The measuring distance of a drum.
How often all night I would lie awake
Too anxious for love, whose map
Is narrow as the bed or tomb,
My spirit's map growing to Europe, gnawed
On her spirit's face by winds of space.
Only the vibrant machine on the sky's skin
Only the emigrant distress on the frontier's rim
Only the iron anger of the Empires
Were symbols of that far reality
Which through the watching door of night
Dissolved the permanence of the city.
Now those warnings of history which the spoiled
Children of the rich exiled
From their great houses and their country lawns
To the unspoken islands of the night,
Return with every wind; and the uncivilized
Insolent message from the barbarian kraal
Across the little middle sea, upon
The yellow staring triangular continent,
Beats out its message in their lives.
I have become
The centre of that clamorous drum
To which I listened all my life

Whose letters spell the time's meaning
In this prison and my death.

THIRD RED and FIANCÉE. Look!

> [*The light in the cell goes out. Enter two of*
> BLACK CHORUS *who take* JUDGE, FIANCÉE
> *and* THIRD RED *away. Enter* BLACK TROOP
> LEADER, *who speaks to the audience from the*
> *front of the stage.*]

BLACK TROOP LEADER. Those who opposed the walls
 of our advancing sea
Are crushed to pebbles. Their minds faded and failed,
O failed and faded like flowers before our enormous
 tide
Whose tall wordless movement does not resemble
 history
Taught in their libraries. For we are in no sense
 ideas:
We do not discuss and cannot be discussed.
Indivisibly we ARE, and by our greater strength of
 being
Defeat all words. Yet this Judge, in the last
 analysis believed
That an argument would govern the state which
 drew its form
From the same sources as the symmetry of music
Or the most sensitive arrangement of poetic words
Or the ultimate purification of a Day of Judgment.
Because our manners did not fit his mental pattern
When, for example, Petra's battered corpse seemed
 unspeakable,

109

Simply, he failed to perceive how far we were serious.
Yes, in his death, his body does not sleep
In a more rigid stupor than when he woke
To the overwhelming reality of our so-called bar-
barousness,
Which to him seemed a nightmare where his time
fell asleep;
For all his life he had sweetly dreamed, and our
awakening
Is his sleeping, our victorious life is his death.
But in our strength lies our seriousness
As in his weakness lay his irresponsibility.
For, in refusing to use it, his like secretly destroyed
The sources of their own power, their over-ripeness
held out a breast
At which the blonde monster, which would destroy
them, fed.
Their cities began to decay; green summer flooded
The last houses and factory yards; the tall sword
grass
Cut at the steel rails of suburban lines.
Like rusting cogs, the tanned, naked unemployed
Lay on canal banks bathed in sun's white wilder-
ness.
In cafés, in darkness, in tenements, in slums, at
street corners,
Voices grew sharp as knives and lives cut their
moorings.
Violence and riot flowered. But now all that is
ended.

The great change has come which means nothing
  will change.
Established power will have power like electricity
Wired through the street by our visible army.
The bank clerk's small house, the peasant's own
  field
Will no longer lie unguarded but be furious pro-
  perty.
Raise an army. Make munitions. Build roads
Leading outwards to our boundaries like the veins
From a heart. But the distended heart is angry
And at last it will burst over Europe as a bomb.
          [*A shooting squad fires behind the stage.*]
                              [*Exit.*]
VOICES FROM CELLS BEHIND THE STAGE.
    But we shall win.
    Look, look!
          [*Enter the Left and Right Hand cells,* CHORUS
          OF RED PRISONERS. *At first they can hardly be
          seen through the darkness which gradually
          lightens, but the stage is never fully light. They
          speak very quietly at first, then their chorus rises
          to a crescendo with the third verse.*]
TWO RED PRISONERS. Fixed in stone darkness where
    we dwell
  With eyes starred in surrounding night
  The chainless freedom of our will
  Burns towards the light.
CHORUS OF RED PRISONERS. O light of day
  The signal be

Of man's release
We shall be free
We shall find peace.

Two Red Prisoners. Far from our friends, children
and wives,
Freedom of light that strikes on leaves,
Our thoughts melt into those whose lives
Suffer the ignorance of the slaves.

Chorus of Red Prisoners. Worker in mine
Our hands that join
The signal be
Strength to increase
We shall be free
We shall find peace.

Two Red Prisoners. Your days in dark, our dark
that wakes,
Across the centuries and the waves
Will join to break our chains and break
Into the nobler day which saves.

Chorus of Red Prisoners. O break of day
The signal be
Of man's release
We shall be free
We shall find peace.

[Eighth Black, Ninth Black *and* Black
Troop Leader *appear at the edge of the stage,
to the extreme right whilst the lights suddenly
illuminate them, and stare in rigid silence at the
prisoners. Whilst the rest of the stage is in semi-
darkness, the walls dividing the three cells collapse,*

112

*forming a sort of gable in the centre of the stage.
During this final stanza of the Chorus, the two
sides of the* CHORUS *meet and join hands across
this obstruction.*]

CHORUS OF RED PRISONERS. Quiet . . . Quiet . . .
Quiet . . .
Whisper of leaves . . . Far, far from laughter . . .
We are betrayed . . . The blackness stares
With bat eyes and furry ears . . .
Softly . . . softly disappear . . .
No sound of strike or riot . . .
Softly . . . softly . . .
Softly . . .

[*Exeunt the* PRISONERS.]
[*Darkness. Then the spotlights reveal* PETRA'S
MOTHER *and the* JUDGE'S WIFE, *pale and
chalky as ghosts, lolling on the gable formed by
the walls of the two outer cells.*]

MOTHER. Paid, paid, all have paid
To their last blood
The price of vanity.
My sons, victims of vanity,
Not for themselves, but vanity
Of the belief that man
Can overthrow systems of injustice
And build systems of justice.
Till their hatred of injustice
Justified tyranny, justified murder
And the cutting away of others' lives
With the will's steel

113

Dividing the good from the waste matter.
Vanity, vanity
Of this judge, seeking integrity
In his own suffering to pierce
The core of humanity.
All, all were vain, yet these
Loved human justice
And lost justice
When the most unjust
And the most violent, won.
Yet the unjust victory
Attains its height of gain to meet
Total defeat.
All actions and all violence fail
Which ignore that God is strong
And man is weak.

    [*She leans back—crumples up almost—in an attitude of complete exhaustion.*]

WIFE. Great sacrifices have been made.
Mothers have given their sons. And
I have given my husband.
For in death he is with us and has become
A hero. His mind
Was terrible, like the soldier's
Who, in the midst of battle, knows fear:
The flag, the slogans, the word of command forsake
    him
And he turns to run, but our officer's saving bullet
Seals his death to our glorious fate:
Yet in that instant his severed heart

Had opened to an eternal truth of terror
Outside our time, realer than all his experience.
My husband had the courage
Of those with the true vision of cowardice
Who dwell amongst the roots of darkness
Compared with which darkness is a flower.
Through what space, amongst what spheres—
It is healthier not to look where he has looked.
[*With real sentiment.*] Therefore, my poor dear lamb
    was sacrificed.
[*Bravely.*] But I comfort myself that his dream has
    come true.
How he would love to have seen
The soldiers march towards the boundaries,
Our men's faces in uniforms all one face,
The face of those who enter a wood
Whose branches bleed and skies hail lead.
And the aeriel vultures fly
Over the deserts which were cities.
Kill! Kill! Kill! Kill!
    [*A low drum, as the lights fade. Then, from be-*
    hind the stage, through the darkness, the whisper
    of the CHORUS *is again heard.*]
CHORUS OF RED PRISONERS. We shall be free.
We shall find peace.
                [*Three loud drum taps.*]
      CURTAIN